THE RAZ/SHUMAKER PRAIRIE SCHOONER
BOOK PRIZE IN POETRY

Editor Kwame Dawes

LET OUR
BODIES
CHANGE
THE SUBJECT

JARED HARÉL

University of Nebraska Press   Lincoln

Acknowledgments for the use of previously
published material appear on pages xi–xii, which
constitute an extension of the copyright page.

The University of Nebraska Press is part of a land-
grant institution with campuses and programs on the
past, present, and future homelands of the Pawnee,
Ponca, Otoe-Missouria, Omaha, Dakota, Lakota, Kaw,
Cheyenne, and Arapaho Peoples, as well as those of the
relocated Ho-Chunk, Sac and Fox, and Iowa Peoples.

∞

Library of Congress Cataloging-in-Publication Data
Names: Harel, Jared, author.
Title: Let our bodies change the subject / Jared Harél.
Description: Lincoln: University of Nebraska
Press, [2023] | Series: The Raz/Shumaker
Prairie Schooner Book Prize in Poetry
Identifiers: LCCN 2023006216
ISBN 9781496237293 (paperback)
ISBN 9781496238283 (epub)
ISBN 9781496238290 (pdf)
Subjects: BISAC: POETRY / Subjects &
Themes / Family | LCGFT: Poetry.
Classification: LCC PS3608.A7288 L48 2023 |
DDC 811/.6—dc23/eng/20230222
LC record available at https://lccn.loc.gov/2023006216

Designed and set in Garamond by L. Welch.

for my parents
and their parents
and theirs

Notice: I say *we*; there, every one, separately,
Feels compassion for others entangled in the flesh

—CZESLAW MILOSZ, "On Prayer" (trans. Robert Hass)

CONTENTS

SOURCE ACKNOWLEDGMENTS

Thank you to the amazing editors of the following journals, in which these poems, sometimes under different titles, first appeared:

Academy of American Poets Poem-a-Day: "January 20, 2021"
American Poetry Review: "As Plagues Go," "Having a Third,"
    "Hold," "Let Our Bodies Change the Subject," "On Suffering,"
    "Our Wedding," "Overnight," "Starfish," "Takeaways"
Arts & Letters: "Every Time I Think My Life Is Hard . . . ,"
    "A Moving Grove"
Asheville Poetry Review: "You Want It Darker (2016)"
Beloit Poetry Journal: "The Great American Eclipse," "Tefillin"
Bennington Review: "The Other Side of Desire"
Defunct Magazine: "All I've Ever Wanted"
Diode Poetry Journal: "Primal," "The Secular among Us," "Spring Crush"
Electric Literature—The Commuter: "The Perimeter"
Four Way Review: "Birthday," "Kin"
Gettysburg Review: "Engaged"
Harvard Review Online: "Good Star"
Laurel Review: "Dolls Can't Talk"
New Ohio Review: "Sad Rollercoaster"
New York Quarterly: "My Grandfather Dreams I Am Dead"
North American Review: "Behind the Painted Guardrail"

Paterson Literary Review: "Cordoba," "Slow Dance"

Ploughshares: "Beer Run," "Final Kindness"

Poets of Queens Anthology: "Along the Path to Washington Irving's House," "My Stupid Pride"

Smartish Pace: "If I Never Find God," "Survival Mode," "Swim Lessons"

Southern Humanities Review: "A Childhood of Nannies"

Southern Review: "Achilles"

The Sun: "Plastic Butterflies"

32 Poems: "Elegy for Recycled Encyclopedias," "Portrait of a Heron"

Thrush: "The Sweet Spot"

Underwater New York: "Water Damage"

Westchester Review: "Self-Portrait as Nature Preserve"

"All I've Ever Wanted," "Let Our Bodies Change the Subject," and "Sad Rollercoaster" were featured in Thomas Dooley's Poetry Well/Emotive Fruition performances.

"Let Our Bodies Change the Subject" and "A Moving Grove" were featured in the Red Door Series in Jackson Heights, New York.

"You Want It Darker (2016)" was awarded the William Matthews Poetry Prize from *Asheville Poetry Review*.

Let Our Bodies Change the Subject

I.

Sad Rollercoaster

My daughter is in the kitchen, working out death.
She wants to *get it*: how it tastes and feels.
Her teacher talks like it's some glittery gold sticker.
Her classmates hear rumors, launch it as a curse
when toys aren't shared. Between bites of cantaloupe,
she considers what she knows: her friend's grandpa lives only
in her iPad. Dr. Seuss passed, but keeps speaking
in rhyme. We go to Queens Zoo and spot the beakish skull
of a white-tailed deer tucked between rocks
in the puma's enclosure. *It's just for show*, I explain,
explaining nothing. That night and the one after,
my daughter dreams of bones—how they lift
out of her skin and try on her dresses. *So silly!* she laughs,
when I ask if she's okay. Then toward the back-end
of summer, we head to Coney Island to catch
a Cyclones game. We buy popcorn and fries. A pop fly arcs
over checkerboard grass when past the warning track,
the park wall, she sees a giant wooden spine,
this brownish-red maze traced in decay. She calls it
Sad Rollercoaster, then begs to be taken home.

All I've Ever Wanted

The almond milk has turned. Flecks of foul snow
slink in slow liquid. Not the discovery
I had angled for this morning, but as my dad
likes to sing like some Jewish Mick Jagger,
You can't always get what you want, which is just
what I croon to my two children, driving them

up the wall because of course all they want
is to get what they want: a fifth scoop
of gelato. To play *Minecraft* till their eyeballs
pixelate in their skulls. What humbling work
to haul kids toward thoughtful—the *kind*
in humankind—like a foreign language

on a stubborn tongue. Yet even as a toddler,
my son would refuse a lollipop if his sister
didn't get one. Still plucks an extra sticker
to gift her after school. And hell, my daughter
can't ride an elevator without making a new friend
or some lady's day by praising her earrings,

her sweater or purse. My point about discovery
has escaped me by now, though I know
the old chorus for thwarted desire. My cereal
will be dry. Coffee taken black. I will try
against hope to be better than myself, which is all
I've ever wanted and everything I need.

The Sweet Spot

On better days, I can tell this is it: we are well
inside it; that *misfortune* implies a fortune

to lose. I can see, despite it all, we have hit
our sweet spot, the best it's gonna get, and yet

someone out there dreams she's a hummingbird,
and is fighting like hell not to wake up.

Overnight

after Nikki Giovanni

A daughter returns to you
with three new freckles
and the purple stain
of popsicle on her tongue.
She gives nothing but what you glean
from slimmed features,
sneakers gone old, the black hole
of a backpack she shrugs
off her shoulders
to race unencumbered
toward her friends
down the street.

Just yesterday she clung
to the nape of your t-shirt,
begging to stay.

Just yesterday
she was yours, and you,

you gave her away.

Beer Run

It was summer. I was small. My uncle plunked me
into his pickup to keep him company
on his run for more beer. I was glad to go.
He was a loud, belching man who killed bugs
for a living. My father's brother, with three golden teeth.
I recall the calm sun: yellow and smeared.
The smell of grill smoke as we rolled down the drive.
The first time I drove drunk I didn't think
I was buzzed. A high school sophomore, I swore
I'd deciphered the curve of every leaf.
Each slow-motion signpost arrowed me home.
Headlights appeared, piercing night's skin,
yet how easy it seemed to weave around them
like a practiced trick, all traffic cleared up.
Years before, I could hear my mom chatting
on the porch, her voice lifting as I sat
in that truck with no backseat, beside my uncle
and green squirt bottles in a cardboard box.
What did I know about fear and preservation?
The sour smell of too many beers? There was a jolt.
A slip. Asphalt under rubber. A patch of daffodils
smiled goodbye. How could I have guessed
why my father was sprinting, screaming after us
down the middle of the street, or why he wouldn't stop
shaking as he ripped me from the truck?

Swim Lessons

To save them from drowning,
we let our children sink
into the arms of an instructor
in the old basement pool
of our local JCC. Once a week
for forty-five minutes, my wife and I
watch on white plastic chairs
as they practice not dying
with mixed results. One lesson,
they learn their bodies must
be violent to stay afloat.
Next lesson, to stay afloat,
they must be perfectly still.
But mostly it's a rash of erratic
splashes. They blow bubbles
and kick in pink and blue
swim caps. Reptilian goggles
press circles into their skin.
Later when they emerge
chlorine-slick and shivering
above the teal-tiled floor,
we wrap them up and swear
how brilliant they were,
which is the lie we recite
before pulling them in.

The Perimeter

My excitement hurts, my daughter sulks
at Columcille Megalith Park, where stones stack
on stones upon a great big stone circling
the sun. It's mid-July, muggy, and my excitement
hurts too, though somewhere along the line
I lost the right to say so. Or the nerve. Or the family
we've traveled with are too damn nice and who are we
to knock anyone's excitement with glazed over
eyeballs, our disinterest in rocks? Instead I tug
my kid to a nearby pond where sorbet-colored koi
curl the perimeter. I once heard koi can live
for two centuries, and so imagine their excitement
must be hurting about now. Then suddenly,
amid the heat and koi and our friends snapping selfies
between some basic-looking archways, my daughter
starts singing. I mean really singing, at the top
of her lungs. All the trees seem to steady
in Bangor, Pennsylvania, until I can feel the soft arc
of our planet in orbit, and dark space like muscle
behind the sky's blue face. And it's true, experience
can be so peculiar—the way it rises like a fish
in still waters, its alien lips agape, gasping
at the air. And here I am, beside myself, gasping.

Plastic Butterflies

Binghamton, New York

Lonely and a little bored,
I used to donate blood every eight weeks
at the Red Cross across the street
from my studio apartment.
Eyes skyward, arm shot straight, I'd sigh
as the butterfly settled on my skin,
its wings drawn to a vein
in my forearm: a thin
river, ghost blue. And then—
warmth. Like an oven turned low, a slow
kindling beneath dark winter clothes.
Afterward I'd pocket Oreos,
fig bars, a few extra juice boxes for later
that night, yet leave feeling lighter,
like I'd done something no one
could diminish. I still donate
here downstate, but last spring,
after the butterfly's sting, I blacked out
in a synagogue basement—
my soaked back on a gurney
as the plastic sack swelled. Nowadays
I can't tell who I'm meant to help,
or how to help, or if anything really helps
anymore, though I guess that's me
feeling lazy and drained
while up north, between two
frozen rivers, a version of my youth
reenters that waiting room
beside a rusted diner and a discount
department store,
lies back, and believes
he has so much more to give.

Takeaways

National Museum of the
U.S. Air Force, Dayton, Ohio

That the military felt it necessary to write BOMB
on its thermonuclear "hydrogen" bomb
might be the greatest argument for never
building one. Here it is: tidy print on a giant green pill
the way I write my son's name inside the collar
of his winter coat, or how my daughter

pilots a pencil between parallel lines. *Takeaways*,
she dubs them—the act of subtraction. I've learned
this country starts us young. Were they nervous
some cadets, fresh from a jog, might think it a scuba tank?
Their long-promised fridge? I made pancakes yesterday
while my son laid waste to our Tupperware cabinet

and his sister dragged graphite through farmhouse cows,
wiping out swing-sets and dolphins and clowns.
There are this many left, she told me, beaming.
Dear Bomb, I can't pretend you aren't impressive—
the science behind you. Your streamlined design.
This impulse to eliminate, name it, say *Mine*.

Elegy for Recycled Encyclopedias

In the end, every detail in the world
couldn't save you. Not a thorough summation
of medieval plumbing systems,
nor the range and migration patterns
of a Eurasian bullfinch. Not Bach, cuckoo clocks,
or even Piaget's theory of object
permanence did the trick. Amid the dim,
dusty heft of entry after entry—each smoke-
stained century, treaty, and canal—there was the hard
data of your being redundant.
A poor use of space. So after decades
insisting you hold post between a La-Z-Boy
and an upright piano, we split the tight ranks
of your regiment, your navy and maroon
uniforms with gold-foil trim.
No, you weren't shocked. You knew all
too well the way of phonographs and monocles,
giant ground sloths and floppy disks.
Grime grew from your uncracked spines
save nostalgia or the occasional
Wi-Fi hitch. It's a miracle that we are
till the instant we aren't. You knew that too—
a knowledge as mythic and
dispensable as fact.

A Moving Grove

A treasure to be told anything true,
though to be fair, it rarely goes well

for the teller. An honest critique
can prove fatal. The botched siege

often taken to heart. In *Macbeth*,
for instance, where news is horrific,

you can feel the messenger break
for ground, shield the delicate bones

of his face before speaking. All year
I've been trying to say something

real, or at least really clever, which
might be my undoing. The kids

want answers about death and God
and if the Muppets are alive and why

is it sunny and when can they stop
hiding in closets at school? It takes

everything in me not to fall on all
fours and cry, *Gracious my Lord,*

I should report that which I say I saw,
But know not how to do it.

Let Our Bodies Change the Subject

In the kitchen, with the kids finally asleep
and news of another shooting
in the space between us,
you confess you think death
might feel like giving birth, the body
insistent, having its way.
You say you'd never been so at the mercy
of yourself as you were on that bed,
in that cloud-thin gown, and just the knowing
it was coming—ruthless
transformation.
   I have no good response
to *ruthless transformation*, and so it hangs there
above a bowl of tortilla chips
and black bean salsa
we've decided will be dinner. It lingers
while a reporter frames chaos
as *developments*, her shoulders rinsed in darkness
and revolving red lights. I want
to kiss you. Build asylum inside you.
Let our bodies change
   the subject, the channel
to cartoons. Before night pulls away
down the flickering interstate,
I want one ruined thing utterly redeemed: a death-
toll rescinded, a swastika removed,
my uncle's melanoma caught early enough
to cut—a beige Band-Aid
halfway down his calf. *It had looked,*
my aunt said, *like little more*
than an ink spot. I didn't get nervous
till it didn't wash out.

II.

Good Star

I swear we hadn't seen a good star in years,
just mild brightenings in a skylined sky
or neon decals on our kids' bedtime ceiling,
until finally we decided to drive upstate
and park beneath a dome of wild darkness.
The baby stayed asleep—a galaxy all his own—
while you sang "Blackbird" upon the curved hood
and our daughter blinked up from the edge
of the field, head back as if rinsing out shampoo.
The night was cold. Her spangly sneakers
went black and still and suddenly I knew
that if we did not reach her, something would—
hushed and hidden, yet I failed to speak.
Then god how I raced to face my reward.

Starfish

aren't fish, in fact,
but marine invertebrates
otherwise called sea stars.
These ancient
opportunistic creatures
fill oceans with little
personality, no
discernible features
but a famed shape.
Still there is something
to say for resilience
in this world.
Lop off a spoke—
not only will the sea star
sprout one back,
but the very bit severed
may grow
a whole self,
its own orbiting star,
an entity entirely
autonomous
and new. And if
this is true, perhaps
each starfish
is the same starfish,
and to eliminate one
you'd have to
flush out the sea.

As Plagues Go

after Natalie Shapero

As plagues go, ten seems excessive.
Consider how the first darkened water

to blood—the mighty Nile gushing
like a giant slit throat. That Pharaoh refused

to relinquish his slaves, and continued
to refuse, says all you need to know

about men + power. But you know what
gets me? How after each plague, when Moses

demanded that the Israelites be released,
God *hardened Pharaoh's heart* to ensure

he wouldn't relent. A divine rigging,
and a pretty dick move. I want to believe

God had His reasons. But I've seen
His kind. All His miracles are crimes.

Achilles

My brother came down with a defensive
rebound in a body prized and trained
against time, much like Achilles
believed he was invincible
until Paris's arrow torpedoed his heel.
Who plunges into battle
without proper footwear? Nearly forty,
my brother wore low-tops—
heard the hard pop of tendon
as he fell. Here on the sofa, his left leg elevated
beside prescription painkillers
and a bottle of blue Gatorade, I strain to stay
casual. Keep things upbeat. I say,
Did you hear there's one Blockbuster left in America?
or, *Achilles actually died of his wound,*
so by most accounts, you're doing really well.
When that fails to take, I challenge
my brother in NBA 2K. We orchestrate
fadeaways, no-look alley-oops—
pixels so intuitive it feels almost true.
But the truth is I don't know
what to do for him. When his best friend,
Patroclus, was killed in battle,
Achilles came out of retirement to avenge
his death—slaughtered Hector,
then dragged his corpse across Troy.
I buy my brother crosswords
and sour gummy worms,
sit through whatever movie he wants to see
as we nurse an ache both sudden
and ancient: these bodies that hold us.
This watching them go.

Hold

A man killed himself
by jumping in front of a Brooklyn-

bound subway while clutching
his five-year-old daughter in his arms.

That the girl survived, somehow
uninjured—though that word

may forever crush against her chest—
is reason enough for me

to hold on, to hold my own
daughter a bit closer this morning

while crossing Queens Boulevard to buy
heirloom tomatoes, or later

at the playground, as her fingertips
grip the monkey bars

above. *Little by little, my love!*
called a woman from the platform

as life crawled out
on her hands and knees.

Along the Path to Washington Irving's House

Tarrytown, New York

There is rain and there is *rain*,
and this is the latter.
It lays upon us heavy and cold
as we scramble up the trail
to the dead author's home.
Undeterred, our daughter splashes ahead.
She pines only for hot cider,
ghost-shaped desserts—
is well-versed in the economy
of obstacle and reward.
But her brother—too toddler to know
this will pass—jams his soaked face
into my shoulder. His arms
tighten, squeezing my throat
as though a rumble of dark hooves
still troubles these woods,
which it does, in a way, gaining
on us. But not before cider.
Not before sweets.

Water Damage

When our basement swamped
for the third time that spring, my father

stepped into the knee-deep muck,
turned, then waited for me

to take his picture, to preserve
this failure of foundation

for insurance purposes, and because
the body, above all, provides

a sense of scale. Right then
we should have known

our house was a sinkhole
that banks would come for, seize

and foreclose. Beneath the polish
of our foyer and cream-tiled

kitchen, black mold rippled
with toxins. Freshly applied paint

bubbled off the walls. But mostly
I recall how my dad looked

in that dank, greenish pool
like a posed child: present

and lost. Or like a spirit risen
after senseless years.

Or exactly like my father, weary
from bailing, emptied

by the flash of all resources
vanished—his reflection

sunk in the stink just below.

A Childhood of Nannies

They ghost through old photo albums
like houseguests who forgot
where they left their coats.
They could be anywhere:
those foreign women who'd coax us
into bathtubs or out of the snow. But now
it's as though each wishes not
to wake us. They toe between pages,
cropped or blinking. Blur
into background, brushing food
off a dish. Only later would I learn
who returned to Guatemala. Who suffered
from lupus. Married or stole.
As a whole, I loved them.
As a whole, I don't know what to do
with the past: all laundered
and folded, tucked in its place.
Irma smelled of hickory. Magdalena
read palms. Dolores had kids
of her own somewhere
and showed us their pictures:
First communion. A missing tooth.
Her babies budding in the arms
of relatives. *Look*, she'd instruct us:
The new haircut. Hand-me-down clothes.
Look. And so we looked.
We got that close.

Excavations in Salemi, Sicily

That summer the U.S. men's soccer team advanced
to the World Cup quarterfinals while Italy fell to South Korea,
we felt a stillness in each piazza—no car horns or celebratory cheers
like the kind that had blasted through Salemi days earlier,
when Italy won. Being American, I didn't give a crap
about soccer. What mattered was that the locals suddenly hated us—
our entire crew—and now refused to let us pickaxe
their crosshatched hillsides, to mine courtyards
for coin and bone. *Name anyone*, they cried. *One player's name!*
They couldn't fathom how a nation that didn't live
for goal kicks and diving headers had surpassed them,
the way a great wave can devastate a house, revise it
into driftwood, and remember nothing. The way none of us—
neither Italian nor American—ever mentioned the war, our *coalition*,
those soldiers dismantling car bombs and driving bullets through bodies
across the Mediterranean Sea. Four days later, we prayed
to be eliminated. We pressed against the glare
of our tiny kitchen television and rooted for Germany,
who beat us 1–0. That night, two locals came by
with a bottle of Calabrese. The shorter man poured
the crimson wine, then informed us, with great ceremony,
we were welcome to resume digging.

The Great American Eclipse

I saw the decapitated sunflower of it
from an arcade parking lot
off Route 110.
My two kids were in there—
giddy, buzzing—
as my mother shoved tokens
into jittery fists. I stepped out—
my head was killing.
I could no longer take
the artificial clinking of ticket dispensers
and mock jackpots
over stained carpet floors. Days before,
I'd been *let go*: a phrase
so passive, so incidental and plain,
like the slightest ease
of fingers from string. I moved
past Laser Tag, past kids drowning
in a pit of plastic balls
and that greased prize counter
like an exhibit for madness. Outside
the August light
had dimmed to ash.
The air felt cooler and rimmed
in stillness like a spacecraft
over Long Island's turnpikes and malls.
I thought of my children
backlit by tilt-screens,
wholly thrilled
to be present and rich.
Then suddenly I rose
up up and away—a small, hollow orb
into darkening skies.

Self-Portrait as Nature Preserve

To believe   at least a piece of me
is worth saving   I slow plod

over twigs   leaves   weave prints
where my body   goes and god

willing will return   with phone
and keys.   Even as we speak

the stream inside me   seems
to run dry   knees like beech

trees calcifying   into quartz.
The kids dart ahead   delighted

to have space   potato chips
packed.   My wife and I

hang back   whisper we can breathe
easier   here.

Then color-   coded markers
bid a footbridge   a lake   a hand-

crafted bench   before bright
mirrored water   that swears:

Devoted Husband,   Loving Father.

Tefillin

You think you know your life till you forget
your own father prays every morning, unzips
a velvet pouch to wrap worn leather strips
about his left arm and hand, seven times around,
like dressing a wound. You forget he prays
in greased blue coveralls before the workday rush
of mufflers and brake pads, and that he prays
on Sundays in sweatpants and socks. He sets
a black box a centimeter above his hairline,
slaps a yarmulke upon his skull, prays, then stops.
You think you know your life but forget
your father has done this since you were six,
since a thin, kindly rabbi spent a week
in your home. How could you forget? It's true
your life no longer confides in you. For too long
you've been wary, screening its calls
like a bookie you have lost all resources
to repay. You forget your father prays the way
he does paperwork—all alone and without
enough light. He never makes a show of it.
Never once offered to teach you how.
You think you know your life until the power
sparks out one snowy December morning,
so you climb your parents' stairs
with your two children and laundry in tow,
and there's a stranger by the curtains—
his eyes squeezed shut, toes arrowed
toward Jerusalem—bound in black lines.

My Stupid Pride

is hard and rusted
as a lug nut—

brownish-red speckles
eating into steel

stripped of its grooves.
I haven't a clue

how to tug it loose,
how to unscrew

this thing I drilled in
so tightly, back

when I swore it
would never undo me.

III.

Behind the Painted Guardrail

My mom and I take my son to Adventureland
to ride every conceivable vehicle
in identical slow circles. We watch
as the firetruck keeps pace with a rocket ship.
An old buggy with the Formula-1 racer.
The park is pretty dead, so she lets him stay on:
this teenage employee with a bright red visor
and a look so vacant it quiets the soul.
As a kid I once proclaimed, *When I get older,
I want to work at Adventureland*, to which my mother
swiftly replied, *When you get older, you want to own
Adventureland!* Turns out I did neither,
but that exchange persists in the annals
of family history as a testament to ambition
and a healthy entrepreneurial spirit.
In truth, my mother knew little about me,
but loved both the me I was and wasn't—
a devotion so bright, I'd vanish in its glow.
My son knows only left turns. He spins
and keeps spinning in his blue police cruiser
before seizing a bulldozer six feet away.
My mom and I wave from behind the painted
guardrail as he sways back and forth, steering
and honking like he owns the place.
The teenager yawns, flips a rusty switch.
I want to tell my mother more than I can say.

My Grandfather Dreams I Am Dead

My mom calls:
the only person

to ever break any
serious news to me.

And naturally
I mishear her, hear

grandpa + dead
and picture front pew

in my Brooks Brothers suit,
a hangman's tie,

the scent of synthetic
lime pressing down.

Then she repeats it:
Your grandfather

thinks you are dead.
I squeeze the cell phone

against my skull.
The sycamores across

the street lean forward
to have a look.

Engaged

Our apartment startled me.
The light of the microwave flushed pink.
I had never known less than I did that morning:
eating cornflakes and late for work.

Weeks blinked by. The hillsides coppered,
then sharpened into view. Jagged pines
lined the freeway. I saw each deer
and the deer saw me.

Before long it was spring. I woke to find you
singing in the kitchen, chopping onions
in nothing but shorts. Made to embrace you,
then remembered the knife.

Cordoba

1.

Long and the color of morning light,
my grandpa kept it tucked
in his one-car garage, draped over
like the newly dead.

When he drove it—
which was seldom—he'd tug
leather gloves down his tailor's fingers,
then sail the neighborhood

slow as a steamer. This was America
for my grandfather—a Jew
from Poland. A Holocaust survivor.
This was about as much freedom

as anyone could bear.

2.

Once, against my will—
for he spoke so little
before failing health softened
his jaw—I rode with him.

A beige seatbelt snaked
my waist. *Don't touch*, he muttered,
mostly to himself.
Still I recall that dashboard

of immaculate switches,
and imagined any one of them
might detonate a townhouse,
or launch us skyward

over wide, suburban streets.

3.
Years later, after his second-
to-last heart attack
forced him to quit driving,
the car was moved

to my parents' yard
where it sat rotting
on deflated tires: a relic.
An eyesore. A pit of wasps

writhed under its hood.
When tow-drivers came,
the Cordoba attacked them—
this rusted sunset

still buzzing: *Don't touch*.

On Suffering

after Wislawa Szymborska

To be clear,
I'm no expert. I know only
that suffering simmers
in every heart, singes in plain sight
like an electric stove.
And though my grandfather told me
over and over, I don't know
how he made it through bone and mud
in some shithole Polish village
in 1941, or how he lost
everything, brutally, and kept
shuffling into light.

Every Time I Think My Life Is Hard, There's Someone in the Sky Reminding Me to Zip It

This morning I see three of them
twelve stories high

on a plank that looks designed

for springboard diving.
I watch them work

in their faded grey sweatshirts

and bright yellow hardhats
tilted toward the sun.

Every time I swear I am never

that brave, I find my son
on my neck, daughter at my sleeve,

each pleading for me

to save them. *Save them.* My life
is easy. I plummet

every time.

Our Wedding

It wasn't what we wanted,
but we wanted each other.

The rest was still something
of a mystery to us.

Still we knew it wasn't
on the four-course menu

or sewn into the fabric
of our expensive rented clothes.

We wanted I think
a lightness, an annunciation

in the trees. In trees we hid
like birds of paradise

waiting for all the tourists
to leave.

Too Soon in San Antonio

after Ada Limón

It's true we trusted a single pink line,
that soft minus sign on the home
pregnancy test that meant, we believed,
we were in the clear. You could order chorizo,
the Tex-Mex special, go horseback riding
through a clumsy ravine. It meant
we could cut loose for our four-day getaway:
pound Dos Equis beside posters
of masked wrestlers, end our nights dizzy,
dumb tourists, stumbling the riverwalk
to track our hotel. It was still early.
We hadn't even told a soul we were *trying*:
that too-intimate and awkward term
that always reminds you of assembling
furniture—of strained instruction manuals
and ill-fitting screws. Of course we knew
our youth was doomed, destined to succumb
to diapers and burp cloths, late-night
feedings before a siege of bad TV.
One picture, in particular, sums that trip up
for me: you like a dream under torn
saloon lighting. And before you, a fishbowl
of golden craft beer! No harm,
thank heavens, but how strange to feel
we should've known. Like we failed
some primal parental exam and ought
to have heard the world's tiniest heartbeat
clicking in darkness, a hitch between Parton
and Petty on the jukebox—our near
and nameless, a different life.

Having a Third

We have two children
but shall not have a third.
A small selfishness, sure,

the way all life choices
imply privilege to choose.
We have two children—

beautiful and bright—
though they fight
like we might only keep one:

the victor of some vital
and ludicrous duel.
We have two children

but won't have a third—
no oops in Aruba.
No minivan in the burbs.

And this fact will shape us
as all inaction must.
No sister for daughter

nor brother for son.
Just two lucky children,
and shadows

between them.

Survival Mode

Our daughter is killing villagers again.
I'm upset because we'd talked about this—
the villager killing—last week over dinner,
and how we're totally not okay with it.
Now here she is, killing villagers again.
It was different this time, our daughter insists,
I just needed somewhere to sleep. She spears
a single green bean, lifts it to her lips.
*You can't get mad at me for needing somewhere
to sleep!* Our son nods along, either listening
or bouncing his bangs into his eyes.
My wife and I glance at each other.
Truth be told, we need more information.
What was she doing roaming a village
with nowhere to sleep? Was killing really
the last reasonable resort? Couldn't
she have bartered, or built her own bed?
We're set to interrogate when our son
suddenly stops bobbing his head to ask
what a villager looks like dead. *Oh,*
says our daughter, setting down her fork.
*You know how dead cows look: all red after they fall
to the ground? Same with villagers. They just die
and that's it. And then they disappear.*

The Secular among Us

My wife stares through me
the way one waits

for a prescription to fill.

Why I vanish over breakfast—
eggs and bacon?—or later

beneath the sci-fi of stars

is difficult to say. *Please,*
I swear, though it's clear

she cannot hear me

like the secular among us
who continue to pray.

If I Never Find God

for and after Baruch &
Yehoshua November

it may be because I search
like how my daughter dawdles
about our modest two-bedroom:

dreamy, off-kilter, driving
me mad, too lucky to really look
for her elusive other shoe.

Final Kindness

Still it feels hateful, filling a grave. To raise dirt
as each spade piles it on. Our task: plug a hole

that holds my best friend's dad. Pack distance
between a corpse and all he cared for.

That the rabbi refers to it as *a final kindness*—
a *mitzvah*—seems amiss, like a door held open

to a room where you are fired. It's early
March and snow is coming—a long shroud

of heavy clouds as we stab at this hill that spills
and resettles. At some point my friend's brother says,

That's enough. The earth nearly level, every collar
flipped up. But his mother—new widow—

who used to chaperone field trips and fix us
lasagna after basketball practice says, *No, finish it.*

So who are we to argue? We keep heaping—
labored breathing—as the thought creeps forth

to bank this as a gym day. It isn't until the first flakes
loosen from sky that we lay down shovels,

dust off our shoes. The ditch has vanished. Like ash
we part to let the grieving party through.

IV.

Portrait of a Heron

You leap off a barstool to take its picture.
You've downed local lagers
with local strangers

and feel the weight of their stories
swimming in your gut.

The air in this country
seems fragrant and holy
and you imagine it towing you
toward the blue ship
of God. But for now you are here
and the bird is *there*—

slim silhouette
against a late spring sunset.
All beak and neck
above soft, bobbing docks.

Then it widens—*such wings*—like everything
you never planned on
passing you by.

Birthday

When my daughter turned seven,
she missed being six.

She didn't want, she said,
to leave her old self behind.

And I, who had turned seven,
then eight, and many more,

sat on the edge
of her warm twin bed

and said, *You take it
all with you, you bring all*

*your selves with you
into the future.* I don't know

what I believe, but I think
she believed me.

I told her nothing is ever lost,
and kept repeating it

till she rose in her nightgown
in the morning dark.

Primal

It seizes   the heart
  not to see   to be seen
dread sprung from centuries
  of being   ambushed
by bushes spear grass
  and caves   which no doubt
hastened us to raise
  walls   forge
weapons any means
  of separation was never enough.
Still what chills
  like   well-
timed darkness? A shadow
  just so?   Each night
I keep the night-
  lights   ablaze
then blame it on the kids.
  I lie awake shove a lacrosse
stick beneath my bed
  in case   some long-
extinct creature thinks
  it can fuck with me.
I think it can fuck
  with me.   I expect
any minute now
  to be taken in its jaws.

You Want It Darker (2016)

The day after the election, Leonard Cohen is dead,
and my eye gets infected, and my daughter
flies around the living room refusing to put on underwear.
I can barely lift my head to see the smug sun
pouring through the blinds, streaming its white spotlight
on each darkened wall. I'm all in on grief and misery.
All in shock and *fuck this country*, but it's still a day, a day
I don't teach, but strap my son into his Cheerio-
encrusted stroller and wheel him to his "baby-taps"
dance class at the Y. We arrive to find the teacher red-eyed
and wrecked, her t-shirt wrinkled, acoustic slung low.
Only one other parent has bothered to show—
her kid wailing beneath the moon-glow of her phone.
When it becomes clear no one else is coming,
the teacher begins to strum and sing of fall, of piggies
at market and monkeys in our beds. We squeeze
our fingers into spinning fists and imagine
we are buses peeling out of town. It all culminates
in the world's saddest rendition of "If you're happy
and you know it," in which we're summoned to rise up
off our multi-colored mats, to clap and stomp
and shout, *Hooray!* Oh, God. Oh, Leonard,
who shed this life like a pinstripe suit, who saw this mess
and chose not to stay, but slip between the bricks
of his Tower of Song, the sun is still out there—
armored and gleaming. There is nothing I can say
to make it stop.

January 20, 2021

This morning the snow
lowered so slowly, I was able
to lift my son—still in pajamas—
and show him each delicate
tendril of frost, the arctic structure
of a solitary flake. I was able
to make coffee and think only
of making coffee, a sensation
so sudden and dangerous
in its delight, I had to dilute it
by burning the toast. This morning
I breathed deeply, clicked on
the television, and watched—
for a moment—a Boeing VC-25 fade
over our capital and dwindle
from sight. Nothing says revenge
like *dwindle from sight*. Later,
I'll hear the new president pledge
to be better, try a bit harder.
I will try to believe him
the way a child believes a father
in an overcoat, by the door.
But for now, all is quiet.
My coffee tastes delicious,
and nothing says revenge like
the stillness of snow.

Spring Crush

It's early spring on our walk home from school
    when my daughter tells me she's in love

with the world. Last week it was a boy
    with small, serious eyes and a glorious bowl cut,

but it seems she's moved on, falling
    for the world as she twirls in its sunlight

and our shadows douse the concrete below.
    Should I aim to dissuade her? Must I explain

this world will leave her for dust, leave her
    with the taste of rust on her tongue? But she smiles

and slips fingers through mine—a sweetness
    not yet teased from her grip. Even those teens

who pack the sidewalk with trendy sneakers
    and covert insecurities stop slap-boxing, pause

to let us pass. Nearly home, we spot blossoms
    burning indigo and pink. A whirl of two squirrels

scrape up a tree. *Better to take things slowly*, I'd say,
    but the girl splits off and sprints

the final block: sun-struck, smitten, a whip of
    perfect limbs stretched to broken sky.

Slow Dance

A *social*, they called it, though we avoided
the girls from the all-girls camp

like they were drugs, or our feelings,
or some invasive species sent to devastate

our lives. They'd step ashore
in ponytails and shorts, intricate lanyards

like licorice around their wrists.
I shudder to think what we looked like

to them: gone weeks without
our mothers or mandatory showers—

a horde of drifters in basketball sneakers
wanting them and wanting them

to go away. Only once all summer
did any of us dance. Our counselors—

sick of our misery, eager to watch
us squirm—shoved us into their bright

chatty packs. One actually smiled at me,
placed her palms on my shoulders,

started to sway. She smelled of bug spray
and strawberry jelly; is a blur

of curls and kindness and skin.
Whatever I hold close begins then.

The Other Side of Desire

What lives inside the body
sleeps there too, builds a nest
of my bones and refuses
to be woken. That I've sunk
into one of my bimonthly ruts
that appear to be a fixture
of adulthood doesn't help.
The kids are the kids, though
suddenly less adorable
when they tickle-attack me
while I sip hot coffee,
or pocket my phone to text
cryptic emojis. Ten years,
and I have lost the ability
to speak with my wife
without a calendar handy—
some future date dying
for design. This is the life
I love and signed on for:
paper hearts and pink glitter
and luck. But one evening
I leave them doing crafts
in the kitchen when at once
something stirs, wants
to know where we're going.

Spring

Each day, fresh evidence
of how thoroughly
I will vanish:

pale petals
on a green puddle.
A deflated foil balloon
mangled in a tree.

I have built this airtight
case against myself.

A jury of my peers
line the sidewalk,
full bloom.

Ruins

If my bones ache
as my son rides a scooter
he does not care to brake

so I must sprint to keep him
from zipping into the street,
is the street my source

of suffering, or my son?
And if later he summons
a stream of tears

for I've restricted his scooter
to fenced-in schoolyards—
small vacant squares—

and if he pleads he indeed
has come to dread death,
what exactly have I won?

And here as I recount
how near I was to ruin—
knees ruined—if I confess

terror casts me as father
to son, like a shadow
that outruns me,

am I well overrun?

Kin

after Joseph O. Legaspi & Larry Levis

Last night my mom called to tell me
I don't call her. I could tell
through the cell phone that each line
was rehearsed. I could tell she was parked
outside Costco or ShopRite
while my father practiced takeoffs
out of Republic Airport—his pale Cirrus
curling the traffic-controlled skies.
Last night my boy beat my ass in UNO—
a barrage of prime numbers
and primary colors, then a Wild + 4
put me to bed. Not bad for a five-year-old
who sleeps cat-like across our pillows
to nuzzle the fantasia of my wife's
midnight hair while I get skull-kicked
by tiny bare feet. My father, a good man,
flies farther from me daily. We see each other
the way a field spots a peregrine
migrating south. My mother left me
another voicemail today. In UNO, the key
is to be free of all cards, to detach
from the very contours of the game.
But I remember after he won
and yelped quietly with delight—
how my son's small hands pressed
the scattered cards together, both together
and toward me to reshuffle the deck.

Dolls Can't Talk

Now that you know your dolls can't talk
and never will no matter how badly

you beg them to, you play with them still
on the living room floor—those half-clad

starlets, pixies, and trolls, a whole militia
of rigid mutes—yet do so with a hint

of concession in your tone, a tolerance
akin to hearing the same story a third

or fourth time, or pretending not to notice
some unpleasant smell. It's an adult skill,

this capacity not to shame, but allow
another the dignity to exist. When did you

learn this? All morning as you animate
plush and plastic—voice giving voice

beyond the crush of static—I've tried
to stay near you, but not interfere,

grading essays or now writing this poem.
Your fingers trace their smug, ageless

faces. How long have you suspected
we might be alone?

NOTES

"All I've Ever Wanted" was written in response to Rosebud Ben-Oni's *Night{Call}* project and her prompt to write a poem that "rethinks the idea of discovery." This poem also makes reference to the Rolling Stones' song "You Can't Always Get What You Want."

"Overnight" is indebted to Nikki Giovanni's powerhouse poem "Allowables."

"Elegy for Recycled Encyclopedias" was inspired, in part, by Pablo Neruda's "Ode to Artichoke."

"A Moving Grove" references William Shakespeare's *Macbeth*. My poem title is lifted from a line uttered to Macbeth by his Messenger in Act V, Scene 5 of the play: "Let me endure your wrath, if't be not so: / Within this three mile may you see it coming; / I say, a moving grove."

"Good Star" makes reference to the Beatles' song "Blackbird."

"Starfish" was inspired by information learned during a family trip to the Long Island Aquarium.

"As Plagues Go" is indebted to Natalie Shapero and many of the poems in her excellent collection *Hard Child*. The poem makes reference to the biblical line: "And the Lord hardened Pharaoh's heart" (Exodus 9:12).

"Along the Path to Washington Irving's House" was inspired by a family visit to Washington Irving's Sunnyside House and refers to Irving's classic story "The Legend of Sleepy Hollow."

"Tefillin" draws on a religious Jewish practice of morning prayers. Tefillin contain a set of black leather boxes and straps with verses from the Torah inside.

"On Suffering" is indebted to Wislawa Szymborska's poem "On Death, Without Exaggeration."

"Too Soon in San Antonio" was prompted by reading Ada Limón's poem "Nashville After Hours."

"If I Never Find God" was inspired by, and is in dialogue with, the poetry of Baruch November and Yehoshua November.

"Final Kindness" is in memory of David Morris, z"l.

"You Want It Darker (2016)" is in memory of Leonard Cohen and refers to his indelible "Tower of Song."

"January 20, 2021" owes a great deal to the friendship and editorial guidance of Joseph O. Legaspi.

"Kin" was inspired by Joseph O. Legaspi's poem "Mothering." My poem's final three lines owe something to Larry Levis's poem "After the Blue Note Closes."

ACKNOWLEDGMENTS

Writing poems can be a strange and solitary endeavor, but I've been lucky to have a tremendous community of family, friends, teachers, and readers along the way.

Thank you to *Prairie Schooner* and the University of Nebraska Press for believing in this book and giving it such an amazing home. Thank you to Kwame Dawes, Major Jackson, and Hilda Raz for this honor and the honor of your attention. Thank you to Sarah Kee, Siwar Masannat, Courtney Ochsner, Rosemary Sekora, Sara Springsteen, Lindsey Welch, and Tryphena Yeboah for your hard work and diligence throughout the publication process. Endless gratitude to Kwame Dawes for editing my book and for your insights and guidance, "step by step."

Thank you to Queens Council on the Arts for supporting this collection with a 2019 "New Work Grant." Thank you to my Diode and BAP families. Thank you to my friends and students at the Writers Circle and NCC and to the many excellent teachers I've had: Elizabeth Wix, Liz Rosenberg, Leslie Heywood, Susan Deer Cloud, Judith Beveridge, Alice Fulton, Kenneth McClane, and Michael Koch.

Thank you to everyone who read early versions of these poems, and this collection, and whose notes helped make this a better book: Will Cordeiro, Jay Nebel, Baruch November, Natalie Shapero, and my APC group—Nancy Agabian, Pichchenda Bao, Catherine Fletcher, Mary Lannon, Meera Nair, and Vaughn Watson.

To my Queens writing community: Jared Beloff, Rosebud Ben-Oni, Francisco Delgado, Nicole Haroutunian, Abeer Hoque, Safia Jama, Olena Jennings, Joseph O. Legaspi, Sahar Muradi, Richard Jeffrey Newman, Sahar Romani, KC Trommer, and many others. And to Queens itself, that beloved borough where most of these poems were dreamed up and jotted down.

Thank you to Téa Obreht, Dan Sheehan, Alexi Zentner, Dan Levine, Ilan Morris, George Mortimer, Rebecca West, and Alejandra Campos for your friendship and support. Thank you to my bandmates, Jeremy and Rob. Gratitude to the editors and friends who encouraged me and sustained my work: George David Clark, Maria Crimi, Thomas Dooley, Jessica DuPont, Jennifer Franklin, Maria Mazziotti Gillan, Sarah Green, Spencer Reece, Elizabeth Scanlon, Matthew Thorburn, David Wanczyk, and BJ Ward.

Thank you to my parents and grandparents for your love and encouragement and for sacrifices I'm only beginning to comprehend. Thank you to my two brothers, my supportive in-laws, my large and expanding family. To Yael, thank you for always being in my corner and for building this beautiful life with me. To Neta and Oren: endless love. I can't wait to see what you'll teach me next.

To order or obtain more information on these or other University of Nebraska Press titles, visit nebraskapress.unl.edu.

Printed in the USA
CPSIA information can be obtained
at www.ICGtesting.com
LVHW040108170823
755391LV00004B/468